Propose a Prefix

Consider This

A **prefix** is a group of letters added to the **beginning** of a word. It changes the meaning of the word.

Prefix	Meaning	Word	Meaning
dis-	not	dislike	not like
un-	not	unable	not able
un-	reverse of	unwind	reverse of wind
re-	again	replay	play again
pre-	before	pregame	before game

Read each sentence. Find the prefix that makes sense.

1 Mrs. Hedaya's 3-year-old girl goes to a ▆school.

2 After the hurricane, the bridge had to be ▆built.

3 If you do not pay your bill, the phone company will ▆connect the phone line.

4 I will ▆tie my ice-skates, then take them off.

5 Before the case is heard by the judge, the lawyer will make some ▆trial arguments.

6 The loss ▆pleased the owner of the team.

7 This pot is too small, so I will ▆plant the flower in a bigger one.

8 The gift was mysterious; its giver was ▆known.

9 The police officer had to ▆able the security alarm before she could enter the bank.

10 I ▆read that book in order to understand it better.

11 The runner was ▆qualified because he started before the bell went off.

12 Sarah left the box ▆opened; she didn't care what was inside.

C re		**E** pre	
A re		**K** un	
J dis		**I** re	
L un		**A** re	
B un		**D** pre	
D un		**H** dis	
E dis		**F** re	
G un		**J** pre	
F pre		**C** dis	
K re		**L** un	
I dis		**G** re	
H re		**B** un	

Objective: Identify correct prefixes, using context clues; understand and practice new vocabulary.

1

All's Well That Ends Well

Consider This

A **suffix** is a group of letters added to the **end** of a word. It changes the way a word is used in a sentence.

Suffix	Meaning	Word	Meaning
-ful	full of	helpful	full of help
-less	without	noiseless	without noise
-ly	like	carefully	done in a careful way
-y	inclined to	cheery	inclined to cheer
-able	able to be	dependable	able to be depended on

Read each sentence. Find the suffix that makes sense.

1 In times of danger, the brave captain always acted fearless▮.

2 The movie was over four hours long; it seemed end▮.

3 A boat that big needs a power▮ motor.

4 The dirt▮ room looked like it had not been cleaned in weeks.

5 The reviewer said that the play was enjoy▮ and that everyone should see it.

6 In the summer, she likes to wear sleeve▮ shirts.

7 The trip went smooth▮; nothing went wrong.

8 The beach is a sand▮ place.

9 That color▮ picture makes the whole room more lively.

10 I hope that dog is train▮; I don't want him to run wild in the house.

11 By eleven o'clock, everyone was sleep▮.

12 That painting is so valuable that people call it price▮.

A y		**B** ly	
D less		**I** ful	
E ful		**F** able	
H less		**A** y	
L able		**D** ful	
G ly		**C** less	
B ful		**H** ly	
I y		**K** less	
F ful		**L** ly	
C ful		**G** able	
K y		**J** ful	
J less		**E** ly	

Objective: Use context clues to identify correct suffixes; understand and practice new vocabulary.

Prefix or Suffix?

Choose the word that has a *prefix*.

1	rewire	patiently
2	disassemble	hopeless
3	itchy	unfamiliar
4	agreeable	remake
5	watchful	unfold
6	presort	carefully

Remember, a prefix is added to the beginning of a word. A suffix is added to the end of a word.

Choose the word that has a *suffix*.

7	unfold	hopeless
8	itchy	disassemble
9	watchful	presort
10	unfamiliar	patiently
11	carefully	remake
12	rewire	agreeable

Answer Box

A	B	C	D	E	F
hopeless	patiently	agreeable	itchy	unfold	carefully
G	**H**	**I**	**J**	**K**	**L**
rewire	remake	disassemble	presort	watchful	unfamiliar

Objective: Discriminate between prefixes and suffixes; understand and practice new vocabulary.

3

Word Chains

Make a word chain. Find the word that forms two compound words.

1 Put the word ■ between sun■town to make sun■ and ■town.

2 Put the word ■ between watch■stand to make watch■ and ■stand.

3 Put the word ■ between base■room to make base■ and ■room.

4 Put the word ■ between head■house to make head■ and ■house.

5 Put the word ■ between home■book to make home■ and ■book.

6 Put the word ■ between bare■ball to make bare■ and ■ball.

7 Put the word ■ between super■place to make super■ and ■place.

8 Put the word ■ between camp■fly to make camp■ and ■fly.

9 Put the word ■ between home■mark to make home■ and ■mark.

10 Put the word ■ between back■stick to make back■ and ■stick.

11 Put the word ■ between out■way to make out■ and ■way.

12 Put the word ■ between sea■line to make sea■ and ■line.

Answer Box

A	B	C	D	E	F
light	yard	work	door	foot	fire
G	**H**	**I**	**J**	**K**	**L**
market	down	ball	land	shore	band

Compound or Not?

Choose the word that _is_ a compound word.

1	watchman	watching	pencil
2	timely	timeline	marking
3	watching	marker	steamboat
4	classroom	pencil	classic
5	marking	bookmark	timely
6	pencil	classic	pigpen

Choose the word that _is not_ a compound word.

7	timeline	timely	steamboat
8	watching	pigpen	watchman
9	pencil	classroom	pigpen
10	bookmark	timeline	classic
11	steamboat	marking	classroom
12	watchman	bookmark	marker

Remember, a compound word is made up of two smaller words.

Answer Box

A	B	C	D	E	F
marker	timeline	watchman	classroom	bookmark	pencil

G	H	I	J	K	L
pigpen	watching	classic	timely	steamboat	marking

Objective: Discriminate between compound words and two-syllable words; understand and practice new vocabulary.

Contraction Match

Complete each sentence. Find the contraction with the same meaning as the words in color.

1 I could not believe my eyes.

2 When I got back from summer camp, my puppy was not the same dog I had left behind.

3 I did not know how much that little dog would grow!

4 My father does not like loud music.

5 My favorite bands were not around when Dad was a child.

6 It is not raining outside.

7 I do not know how to get to Sommerville.

8 That store will not accept checks.

9 You should not try to skate on that thin ice.

10 I would not go skating there today.

11 There are not enough books for the whole class.

12 I have not mowed the lawn this week.

> The contraction <u>won't</u> is special. It is formed from the words <u>will</u> and <u>not</u>.

Answer Box

A	B	C	D	E	F
weren't	aren't	haven't	won't	don't	wouldn't

G	H	I	J	K	L
didn't	shouldn't	isn't	wasn't	doesn't	couldn't

To Be or Not To Be?

Find the contraction with the same meaning as the words in color.

1 I **had not** worked at the Jungleland Animal Park until last summer.

2 **It is** a fun place to work.

3 **They have** added a few new attractions since last year.

4 **We have** waited a long time to go to Jungleland.

5 **They are** better than last year's advertisements.

6 George **has not** come to Jungleland yet.

7 **I am** excited by some of the changes in the acts.

8 **She is** the best animal trainer at the park.

9 **He is** a good trainer, too.

10 **There is not** a better show in town.

11 **We are** sure you will like your trip to Jungleland.

12 **I have** recommended this place to everyone.

Answer Box

A	B	C	D	E	F
It's	hasn't	We're	They're	hadn't	We've

G	H	I	J	K	L
I've	She's	They've	He's	I'm	isn't

Objective: Identify contractions formed with pronouns and verbs, or verbs and the word <u>not</u>; understand and practice new vocabulary.

Contraction Confusion

Read the story. Choose the word shown in color that makes sense.

1 It's, Its not easy starting your own band. If you think it's easy, **2** your, you're wrong.

First, you need to learn the music and practice playing **3** you're, your instrument. Then, your band needs to plan **4** its, it's act. Finally, **5** you've, we've got to find someone who will hire you.

Ben and his friends found out how hard it is. **6** They're, Their starting a new band. Ben says **7** he's, his never worked so hard in his life.

I was **8** there, their when he got his first audition. He asked all **9** he's, his friends to come to show **10** they're, their support. The band played well at the audition, but they **11** we're, were not hired. It was sad to hear them tell Ben, **12** "We're, Were sorry, but your band is not our first choice."

Answer Box

A	B	C	D	E	F
were	you've	he's	their	there	We're
G	**H**	**I**	**J**	**K**	**L**
his	your	its	It's	you're	They're

Objective: Use context clues to discriminate between contractions and
words that sound like contractions; understand new vocabulary.

Magical Synonyms

Read the story. Find the <u>synonym</u> for each word in color.

The Great Zampano is one of the **1** best magicians in the world. I have gone to see him **2** many times over the years. Each time I watch Zampano's act, I see something **3** new.

Tickets for Zampano's shows are always **4** scarce. That's because people **5** start buying them long before the show. To get a ticket, you need to be very **6** early and very **7** lucky. Or, you need to have a **8** friend who is working on the show.

Even Zampano's biggest **9** critic has said some nice things about the act. Once, he said that Zampano could make **10** ancient tricks seem new. If your **11** toughest critic says something that **12** nice, you must be doing something right.

Answer Box

A	B	C	D	E	F
fortunate	old	begin	hardest	pal	pleasing
G	**H**	**I**	**J**	**K**	**L**
greatest	few	novel	judge	timely	several

Objective: Identify synonyms for words, using context; understand and practice new vocabulary.

The Opposite Puzzle

Read each clue. Find its <u>antonym</u> in the crossword puzzle.

Across

1 ugly

3 slow

5 sad

9 ashamed

11 seldom

12 dull

Down

2 wise

4 bland

6 clean

7 mighty

8 huge

10 remain

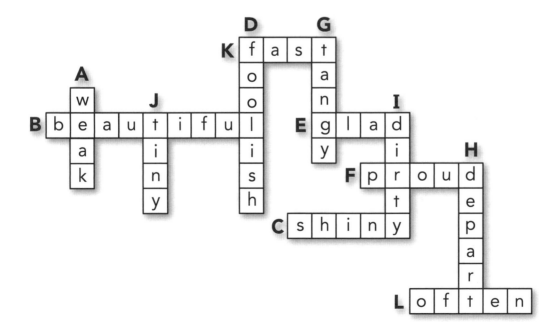

Objective: Identify antonyms for words; understand and practice new vocabulary.

Puzzle Time

Use the puzzle to find the word that matches each clue.

Across

4 antonym for big

7 antonym for ill

8 synonym for ill

10 antonym for shrink

11 synonym for silent

12 synonym for purchase

Down

1 synonym for drop

2 antonym for grow

3 synonym for big

5 antonym for purchase

6 antonym for fall

9 antonym for silent

Answer Box

A	B	C	D	E	F
sick	rise	expand	small	quiet	large
G	**H**	**I**	**J**	**K**	**L**
shrink	buy	fall	well	noisy	sell

Objective: Identify synonyms or antonyms for words; understand and practice new vocabulary.

Identifying Idioms

Match each idiom in color with its meaning.

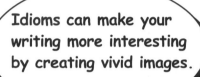

Idioms can make your writing more interesting by creating vivid images.

1 Matt has trouble dancing; he has two left feet.

2 That kind of question is out of bounds; we just won't answer it.

3 That's a horse of a different color; it changes things completely!

4 Sam will bail out the team; he's gotten them out of tight spots before.

5 That number sounds like it's in the ballpark; we can use it as an estimate.

6 Mark was worried; he felt like he was behind the eight ball.

7 Sarah was in a haze; she had almost no idea about what was going on.

8 The company had had a good year; it was in the black.

9 After his first hit CD, the singer felt like he was at the top of the heap.

10 The store had very few customers; it was in the red.

11 That restaurant is at the bottom of the barrel; I never want to eat there again.

12 The computer is on the blink; I need to get it fixed.

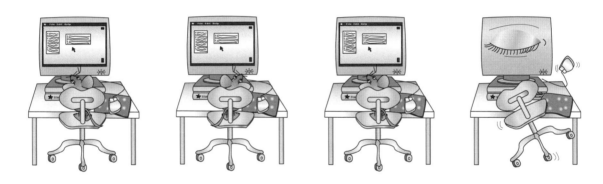

Answer Box

A	B	C	D	E	F
close to accurate	the worst	not working properly	making money	confused	losing money

G	H	I	J	K	L
the best	different situation	not allowed	in trouble or under pressure	is clumsy	save

Objective: Identify idioms and then match them with meanings, using context clues.

13

Welcome to Massachusetts!

Look at this diagram of the state government of Massachusetts.

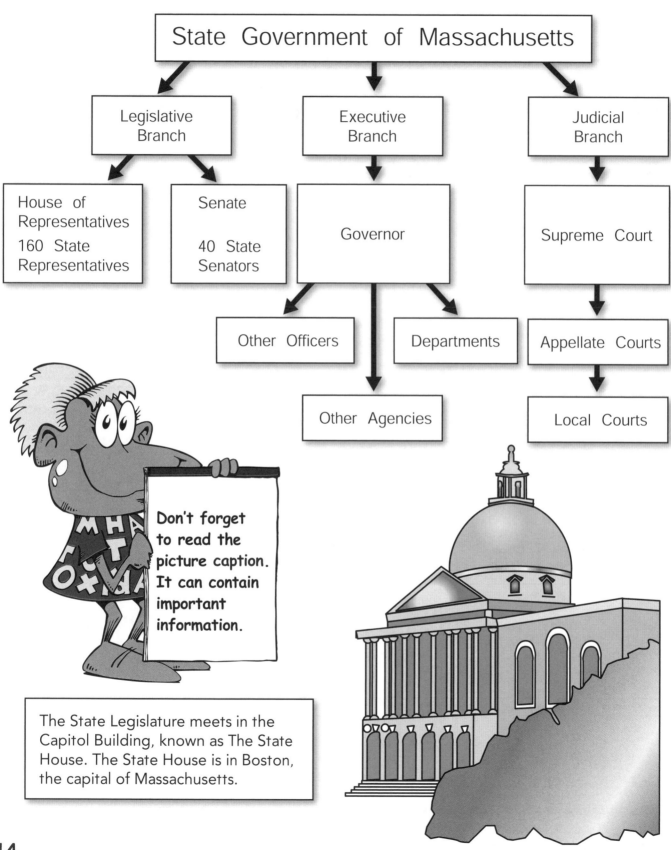

State Government of Massachusetts

Legislative Branch

Executive Branch

Judicial Branch

House of Representatives
160 State Representatives

Senate
40 State Senators

Governor

Supreme Court

Other Officers

Departments

Appellate Courts

Other Agencies

Local Courts

Don't forget to read the picture caption. It can contain important information.

The State Legislature meets in the Capitol Building, known as The State House. The State House is in Boston, the capital of Massachusetts.

Now use the diagram and the caption to find the word that completes each sentence.

1 The House of Representatives is part of the ▪ Branch.

2 The Governor is the head of the ▪ Branch.

3 The highest court in the state is the ▪ Court.

4 Massachusetts has 40 ▪.

5 The second-highest courts in the state are called the ▪ Courts.

6 Massachusetts has 160 ▪.

7 The local courts are part of the ▪ Branch.

8 Other Officers and ▪ report to the Governor.

9 The State Legislature meets in the ▪, which is known as The State House.

10 The state government of Massachusetts has three ▪.

11 The capital city of Massachusetts is ▪.

12 Other Agencies report to the ▪.

Answer Box

A	B	C	D	E	F
State Senators	Legislative	Departments	Governor	Supreme	Capitol Building
G	**H**	**I**	**J**	**K**	**L**
branches	Judicial	Executive	State Represent- atives	Boston	Appellate

Objective: Read diagrams and captions and use them to gather information.

15

Native American Words

Find the word that matches each picture.

1  **2** 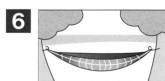 **3**

4 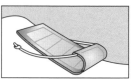 **5**  **6**

Surprised? All of these common words come from Native American culture.

Find the word that fits each definition.

7 hut made by covering poles with hides, matting, or bark

8 Native American corn

9 outdoor feast during which food is cooked over an open fire

10 meeting, conference, or ceremony

11 tropical cyclone

12 dome-shaped house, usually built of blocks of packed snow

canoe
hammock
barbecue
hurricane

Answer Box

A	B	C	D	E	F
toboggan	powwow	barbecue	kayak	hammock	maize

G	H	I	J	K	L
wigwam	totem	hurricane	tomahawk	igloo	moccasin

Objective: Identify words derived from Native American culture that match pictures and definitions.

Words from Spanish and French

Choose the word in color that completes each sentence.

1 If I get tired in the afternoon, I take a (siesta, corral).

2 We all went to the (lasso, rodeo) to see the cowboys compete.

3 My grandfather lives on a big (ranch, fiesta) that has lots of horses.

4 The (rodeo, corral) is the place where Grandfather keeps his horses.

5 On my birthday, my friends will come to my (fiesta, siesta).

6 The cowboy uses a (lasso, ranch) to catch horses.

7 My rich uncle lives in a (mansion, gourmet) that has many rooms.

8 Uncle Emil has a (garden, chef) named Hugo who prepares all his meals.

9 Hugo prepares (mansion, gourmet) food.

10 There is also a (butler, flower) who takes care of many household tasks.

11 Emil has a (garden, butler) that is full of rare plants.

12 The most beautiful kind of (flower, chef) is an orchid.

Knowing where words come from can increase your word knowledge and help you understand spelling patterns.

Answer Box

A	B	C	D	E	F
lasso	rodeo	corral	siesta	ranch	gourmet
G	**H**	**I**	**J**	**K**	**L**
flower	chef	mansion	butler	fiesta	garden

Objective: Identify words derived from Spanish and French, using context and prior knowledge.

Mathematical Meanings

Find the math word that fits the definition.

1 a box with 6 congruent sides

2 the answer in division

3 the distance around a figure

4 a length equal to 12 inches

5 lines in the same plane that never meet

6 the number beneath the line in a fraction

7 a rectangle with 4 equal sides

8 the number above the line in a fraction

9 lines that form a right angle when they meet

10 a length equal to 3 feet

11 the answer in multiplication

12 a figure shaped like a ball

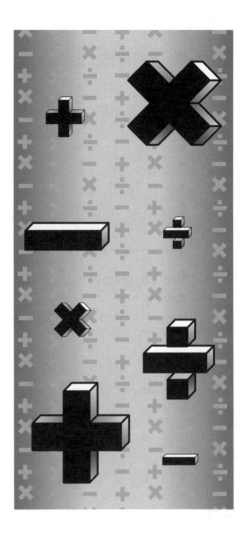

Answer Box

A	B	C	D	E	F
perpendicular lines	perimeter	sphere	numerator	foot	cube
G	**H**	**I**	**J**	**K**	**L**
parallel lines	product	quotient	denominator	yard	square

Objective: Match math-related vocabulary words with their definitions; understand and practice new vocabulary.

Words from Greek and Latin

Use the puzzle to find the
word that matches each clue.

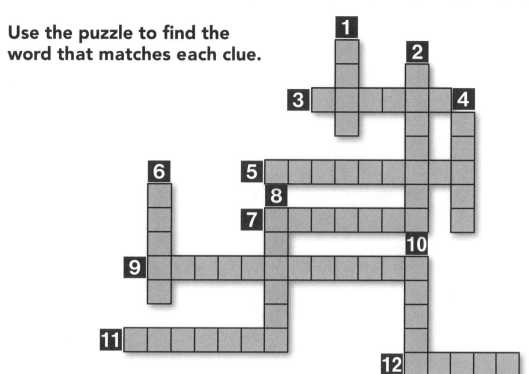

Across

3 literature consisting of poems

5 study of money and wealth

7 to make larger

9 science of designing buildings and other structures

11 those whose job is to edit

12 the facts

Down

1 scientific term for a very small particle

2 natural force that draws objects toward the center of the earth

4 a rhythmic combination of sounds

6 permitted by the law

8 basic units of length in the metric system

10 to burst forth suddenly or violently

Answer Box

A	B	C	D	E	F
legal	gravity	architecture	poetry	music	atom

G	H	I	J	K	L
meters	truth	economics	editors	erupt	magnify

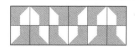

Objective: Identify words derived from Greek and Latin, using definitions and prior knowledge.

19

Take a Close Look

Look at these diagrams of the human eye.

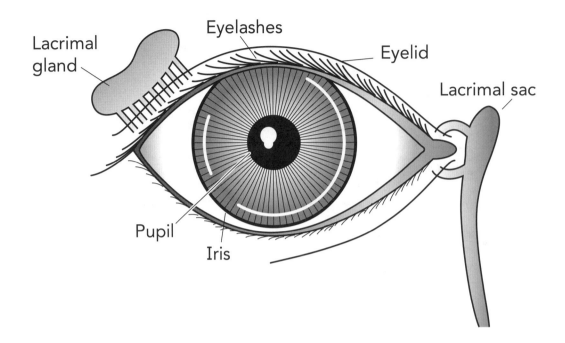

Lacrimal gland

Eyelashes

Eyelid

Lacrimal sac

Pupil

Iris

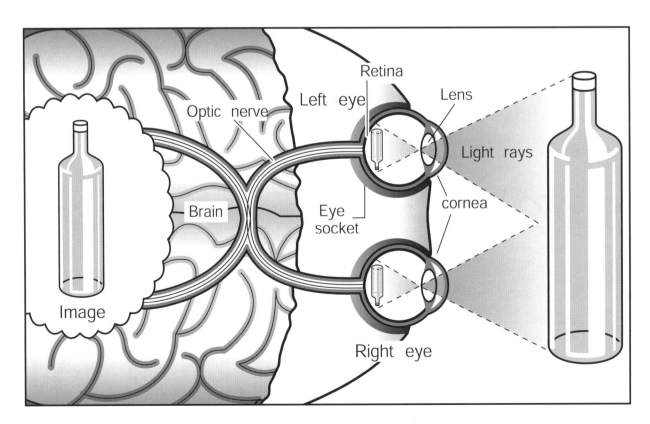

Retina

Left eye

Lens

Optic nerve

Light rays

Brain

Eye socket

cornea

Image

Right eye

Now read each sentence about the eye. Find the name on the diagram that completes the sentence.

1 The entire eye is protected by the ■, which can close over the eye.

2 The ■ is a round opening in the middle of the iris.

3 The ■ on the eyelids help keep dust and other particles from entering the eye.

4 The eyeball is in the ■.

5 The ■ is a colored disk that has a pupil in the middle.

6 The ■, which are above the eyes, produce tears.

7 Tears flow into the ■, located in the corner of each eye.

8 Light rays hit the ■ first.

9 After light rays pass through the cornea, they hit the ■.

10 The lens bends light rays together so that they form a clear image on the ■.

11 The eyes send messages through the ■ to the brain.

12 An ■ forms in the brain.

I can see clearly now!

Answer Box

A	B	C	D	E	F
eyelid	lacrimal sac	pupil	lacrimal glands	lens	iris
G	**H**	**I**	**J**	**K**	**L**
retina	eye socket	image	cornea	optic nerves	eyelashes

Objective: Read diagrams and use them to locate information.

Sight and Sound

Choose the term that describes the musical instrument.

1

   G wind instrument   **D** stringed instrument   **I** percussion instrument

2

   A percussion instrument   **E** wind instrument   **L** stringed instrument

3

   B percussion instrument   **K** stringed instrument   **F** wind instrument

4

   J stringed instrument   **C** percussion instrument   **H** wind instrument

5

   L wind instrument   **A** stringed instrument   **D** percussion instrument

6

   F percussion instrument   **C** wind instrument   **B** stringed instrument

Consider This

Here are some words that are used to describe works of art.

Mural: a painting or decoration that covers all or part of a wall

Portrait: a painting of a person, especially of the face

Collage: a picture or design made by pasting objects such as newspaper, cloth, or cardboard onto a canvas or another surface

Sculpture: a figure that is cut, carved, modeled, or cast from stone, wood, clay, or metal

Now choose the term that describes the piece of art.

7   **B** mural   **D** collage   **I** portrait

8    **A** sculpture   **G** mural   **K** collage

9    **E** collage   **C** mural   **G** sculpture

10    **L** mural   **J** sculpture   **I** portrait

11   **K** portrait   **E** mural   **H** collage

12   **F** collage   **J** mural   **H** sculpture

Objective: Identify correct terms for musical instruments and specific art forms; understand and practice new vocabulary.

23

Computer Words

Read this table of definitions for the parts of a computer.

Part	Definition
CD-ROM	Compact Disk – Read Only Memory; flat plastic disk used to store information digitally
CPU	Computer Processing Unit: the main part of the computer; has the power to store and run programs
cursor	a blinking light that shows where you will type next on the screen
hardware	the parts of a computer that you can see and touch, such as the monitor, printer, and keyboard
joystick	a stick used to play computer games
keyboard	keys representing letters, numbers, and figures; used for entering information into a computer
modem	a device that connects computers through telephone lines
monitor	the screen that shows the computer program
mouse	a device that allows you to move the cursor on the monitor
printer	a machine that prints information from a computer
scanner	a machine that can "read" information on paper into a computer
software	instructions or programs that tell the computer how to do its work, such as for word processing and computer games

Choose the word in color that matches each picture.

mouse **or** joystick

CD-ROM **or** CPU

monitor **or** printer

monitor **or** modem

mouse **or** keyboard

scanner **or** joystick

Choose the word in color that best completes each sentence.

7 The monitor, the computer, and the printer are all examples of (software, hardware).

8 Word processing programs, computer games, and graphics programs are all examples of (software, hardware).

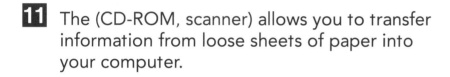

9 The (printer, cursor) shows where you will type next on the screen.

10 The (CPU, keyboard) is a place where you store computer documents and programs.

11 The (CD-ROM, scanner) allows you to transfer information from loose sheets of paper into your computer.

12 The (cursor, modem) connects your computer to a phone line.

Answer Box ·

A	B	C	D	E	F
printer	joystick	cursor	keyboard	mouse	CD-ROM
G	**H**	**I**	**J**	**K**	**L**
software	modem	scanner	monitor	CPU	hardware

Objective: Show an understanding of new vocabulary (computer terms), using definitions, context, and prior knowledge.

25

Street Safety

Find the word or phrase that matches each sign.

1

2

3

4

5

6

7

8

9

10

11

12

Answer Box

A	B	C	D	E	F
no U turn	U turn	left turn only	no pedestrians	no left turn	winding road

G	H	I	J	K	L
pedestrian crossing	no bicycles	deer crossing	stop ahead	hill	road is slippery when wet

Objective: Identify the meanings of street safety signs; understand information presented graphically.

Be Careful!

Choose the place where you are more likely to read each direction.

1 Do not get in eyes.
a container of cleaning fluid **or**
a box of teacups

2 No lifeguard: Swim at own risk.
a front yard **or** a beach

3 Keep out of reach of children.
an abandoned building **or**
a bottle of medicine

4 Fragile: Handle with care.
a box of teacups **or** a front yard

5 Enter at own risk.
a bottle of medicine **or**
an abandoned building

6 Beware of dog.
a front yard **or** a beach

Match each direction with an explanation of what the direction is telling you.

7 Do not ingest.

8 Danger: Thin ice.

9 Caution: Flammable.

10 Do not exit: Alarm will sound.

11 Do not take more than
recommended dose.

12 Do not leave valuables unattended.

Answer Box

A	B	C	D	E	F
a box of teacups	a container of cleaning fluid	a front yard	Do not walk or skate here.	a bottle of medicine	Be careful because contents could catch fire.

G	H	I	J	K	L
Do not swallow or inhale.	Use this door only in times of emergency.	Take your belongings with you when leaving your seat.	a beach	an abandoned building	Follow the directions when taking this drug.

Objective: Show an understanding of commonly seen words of precautions; understand and practice new vocabulary.

27

Follow the Directions

Choose the place where you are more likely to read each direction.

1 Order here.

a sandwich store **or** a highway

2 Fasten seat belt.

an airplane **or** a zoo

3 Keep refrigerated.

an airplane **or** a package of cheese

4 Use before this date.

a carton of milk **or** a cash register

5 Form line here.

a movie theater **or**
a package of cheese

6 Don't walk.

a library **or** a street corner

7 Quiet please.

a library **or** a sandwich store

8 Express: 10 items or less.

a cash register **or** a movie theater

9 Use right lane for carpools.

a highway **or** an airline terminal

10 Do not feed animals.

a carton of milk **or** a zoo

11 Claim luggage here.

an airline terminal **or**
an amusement park

12 Children under 10 must be
accompanied by an adult.

an amusement park **or**
a street corner

Answer Box

A	B	C	D	E	F
a carton of milk	a sandwich store	a movie theater	a highway	a street corner	an airplane
G	**H**	**I**	**J**	**K**	**L**
a zoo	a library	a package of cheese	an airline terminal	a cash register	an amusement park

Objective: Show an understanding of the meanings and uses of imperative
directions; understand and practice new vocabulary.

Watch the Signs!

Find the sign that answers each question.

1 Which sign tells you that you can leave but not enter through this door?

2 Which sign tells you that dogs are not allowed?

3 Which sign tells you that there is no parking allowed?

4 Which sign tells you that traffic goes only in one direction?

5 Which sign tells you that there are no more tickets left for a particular show?

6 Which sign tells you that a street doesn't take you to another street?

7 Which sign tells you how fast you can drive?

8 Which sign tells you to use this door in case of a fire?

9 Which sign tells you the hours for a store that is open every day of the week?

10 Which sign tells you that you are leaving or entering a state?

11 Which sign tells you the hours for a store that is open every day of the week but Sunday?

12 Which sign tells you that parking is for persons with disabilities?

Answer Box

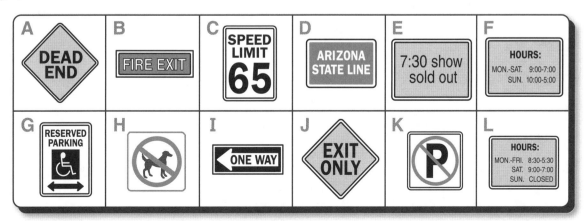

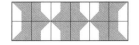

Objective: Show an understanding of the meaning of the graphic information presented on signs.

Words That Relate

Consider This

Analogies explore relationships. They are a kind of comparison.

 is to U turn as is to no U turn.

In this analogy, the relationship between the first sign and the words "U turn" is similar to the relationship between the second sign and the words "no U turn."

Find the word or phrase that completes each statement.

1 is to train station as is to ▮.

2 is to no trucks as is to ▮.

3 is to right turn only as is to ▮.

4 is to library as is to ▮.

5 is to no right turn as is to ▮.

6 is to bicycle crossing as ▮ is to ▮.

Find the symbol that completes each statement.

7 Library is to as marina or boat docks is to ■.

8 Train station is to as bus station is to ■.

9 Bicycle crossing is to as pedestrian crossing is to ■.

10 No right turn is to as no left turn is to ■.

11 No trucks is to as no pedestrians is to ■.

12 Right turn only is to as left turn only is to ■.

Answer Box . . . .

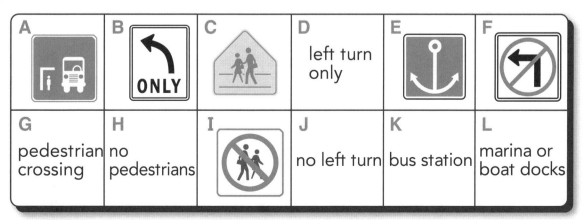

Objective: Show an understanding of symbols and the words that represent them by completing analogies.

Make the Connection

Find the word that completes each statement.

1 Listen is to music as view is to ▪.

2 Minute is to clock as inch is to ▪.

3 Garden is to flowers as forest is to ▪.

4 Finger is to hand as toe is to ▪.

5 Wheel is to bicycle as blade is to ▪.

6 Degree is to thermometer as pound is to ▪.

7 Stable is to horses as pen is to ▪.

8 Purr is to cat as roar is to ▪.

9 Crayon is to draw as pencil is to ▪.

10 Hot is to fire as cold is to ▪.

11 Lawyer is to court as doctor is to ▪.

12 Chef is to kitchen as teacher is to ▪.

Think about how the first pair of words goes together. Then find the word that makes the second pair of words like the first.

Answer Box

A	B	C	D	E	F
hospital	skate	ice	foot	lion	school
G	**H**	**I**	**J**	**K**	**L**
trees	write	painting	pigs	scale	ruler

Objective: Show an understanding of the meanings of words by completing analogies.